PRIMARY MATHEMATICS 2A
TEXTBOOK

Marshall Cavendish Education

SingaporeMath.com Inc

Original edition published under the title Primary Mathematics Textbook 2A

© 1982 Curriculum Planning & Development Division

Ministry of Education, Singapore

Published by Times Media Private Limited

This American Edition

© 2003 Times Media Private Limited

© 2003 Marshall Cavendish International (Singapore) Private Limited

Published by Marshall Cavendish Education

An imprint of Marshall Cavendish International (Singapore) Private Limited

Times Centre, 1 New Industrial Road, Singapore 536196

Customer Service Hotline: (65) 6411 0820

E-mail: fps@sg.marshallcavendish.com

Website: www.marshallcavendish.com/education

Distributed by

SingaporeMath.com Inc

404 Beavercreek Road #225

Oregon City, OR 97045

U.S.A.

Website: http://www.singaporemath.com

First published 2003

Second impression 2003

Third impression 2004

Reprinted 2004

Fourth impression 2005

Reprinted 2005

Fifth impression 2006

Reprinted 2006, 2007, 2008, 2009 (twice), 2010

ISBN 978-981-01-8498-8

Printed in Singapore by Times Printers, www.timesprinters.com

ACKNOWLEDGEMENTS

Our special thanks to Richard Askey, Professor of Mathematics (University of Wisconsin,
Madison), Yoram Sagher, Professor of Mathematics (University of Illinois, Chicago), and Madge
Goldman, President (Gabriella and Paul Rosenbaum Foundation), for their indispensable
advice and suggestions in the production of Primary Mathematics (U.S. Edition).

PREFACE

Primary Mathematics (U.S. Edition) comprises textbooks and workbooks. The main feature of this package is the use of the **Concrete** ➡ **Pictorial** ➡ **Abstract** approach. The students are provided with the necessary learning experiences beginning with the concrete and pictorial stages, followed by the abstract stage to enable them to learn mathematics meaningfully. This package encourages active thinking processes, communication of mathematical ideas and problem solving.

The textbook comprises 6 units. Each unit is divided into parts: ❶, ❷, . . . Each part starts with a meaningful situation for communication and is followed by specific learning tasks numbered 1, 2, . . . The textbook is accompanied by a workbook. The sign Workbook Exercise ⟩ is used to link the textbook to the workbook exercises.

Practice exercises are designed to provide the students with further practice after they have done the relevant workbook exercises. Review exercises are provided for cumulative reviews of concepts and skills. All the practice exercises and review exercises are optional exercises.

The color patch ■ is used to invite active participation from the students and to facilitate oral discussion. The students are advised not to write on the color patches.

CONTENTS

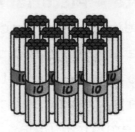

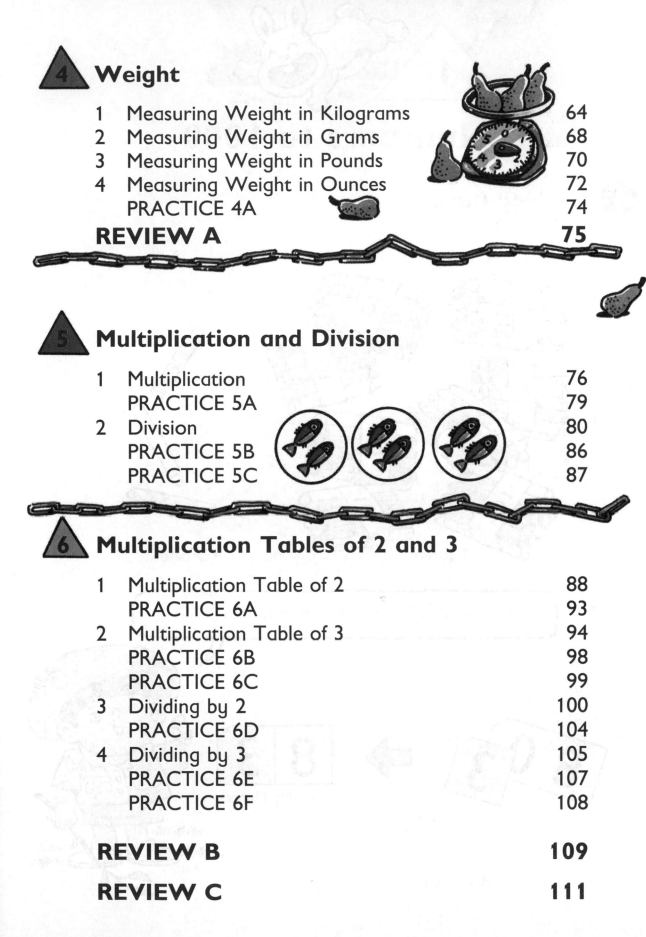

1

Numbers to 1000

1 Looking Back

8 tens

3 ones

How many crayons are there altogether?

8 0 3 → 8 3

eighty-three

80 and 3 make 83.

6

1. (a) How many mangoes are there?

   (b) 40 and 5 make ▮ .

   (c) 5 more than 40 is ▮ .

   (d) 40 + 5 = ▮

2. How many stamps are there?

Count by tens:
10, 20, 30, 40, 50,
60, 70, 80, 90, 100

10 tens make 1 hundred.

3. Count the tens and ones.

(a)

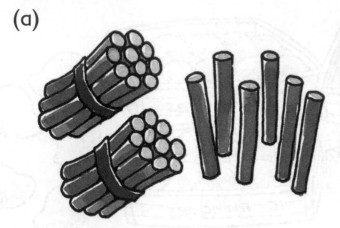

Tens	Ones
2	6

twenty-six

2 tens   6 ones =

(b)

Tens	Ones
4	3

forty-three

4 tens   3 ones =

(c)

Tens	Ones
5	7

fifty-seven

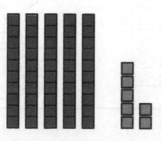

tens ones =

Workbook Exercise 1

4.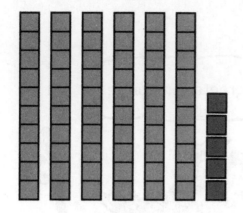

Tens	Ones
6	5

5 more than 60 is 65.

(a) What number is 1 more than 65?

(b) What number is 1 less than 65?

(c) What number is 10 more than 65?

(d) What number is 10 less than 65?

5. (a) What number is 2 more than 65?

(b) What number is 2 less than 65?

(c) What number is 20 more than 65?

(d) What number is 20 less than 65?

6. (a) $80 + 1 =$ ☐   (b) $80 + 2 =$ ☐

(c) $80 + 10 =$ ☐   (d) $80 + 20 =$ ☐

(e) $80 - 1 =$ ☐   (f) $80 - 2 =$ ☐

(g) $80 - 10 =$ ☐   (h) $80 - 20 =$ ☐

9

Workbook Exercise 2

2 Comparing Numbers

I always take the greater amount.

21 is greater than 12.

We write : **21 > 12**

99 is less than 100.

We write : **99 < 100**

This sign means **greater than**.

This sign means **less than**.

1. Which sign would you use, > or <?

(a)

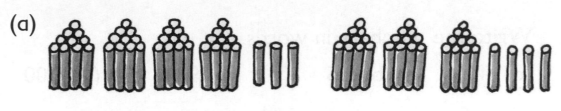

43 ● 34

(b)

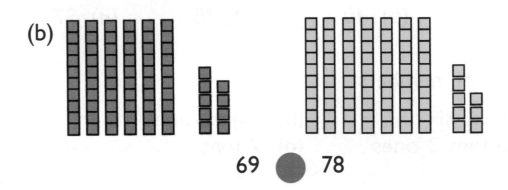

69 ● 78

(c) 35 ● 32   (d) 29 ● 37

(e) 47 ● 50   (f) 50 ● 49

2. (a) Which number is smaller, 40 or 39?

(b) Which number is greater, 29 or 30?

(c) Which number is the smallest, 65, 64 or 56?

(d) Which number is the greatest, 89, 90 or 98?

3. Arrange the numbers in order.
Begin with the smallest.

59   95   90   50

PRACTICE 1A

1. Write the numbers in words.

   (a) 44   (b) 55   (c) 95   (d) 100

2. Write the numbers in tens and ones.

   (a) 65   (b) 40   (c) 78   (d) 97

3. Write the numbers.

   (a) sixty-six   (b) eighty-one
   (c) 5 tens 3 ones   (d) 7 tens

4. (a) What number is 4 more than 50?

   (b) What number is 3 more than 70?

5. (a) What number is 1 more than 99?

   (b) What number is 1 less than 50?

6. (a) What number is 10 more than 79?

   (b) What number is 10 less than 45?

7. Which sign would you use, > or <?

   (a) 34 ⬤ 29   (b) 89 ⬤ 90

   (c) 46 ⬤ 45   (d) 71 ⬤ 70

   (e) 105 ⬤ 100   (f) 50 ⬤ 52

12

③ Hundreds, Tens and Ones

I bundle the straws in tens. Then I put 10 tens together to make a hundred.

Count by hundreds.

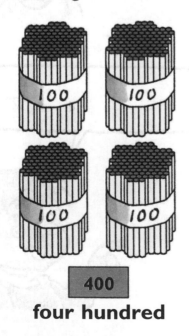

100 100
100 100

400

four hundred

100, 200, 300, 400

13

Count the straws.

100, 101, 102, 103, 104, 105, 106

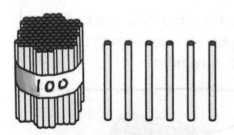

106

one hundred six

100, 110, 120, 130, 140

140

one hundred forty

100, 200, 210, 220, 221, 222, 223

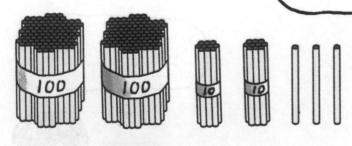

223

two hundred twenty-three

14

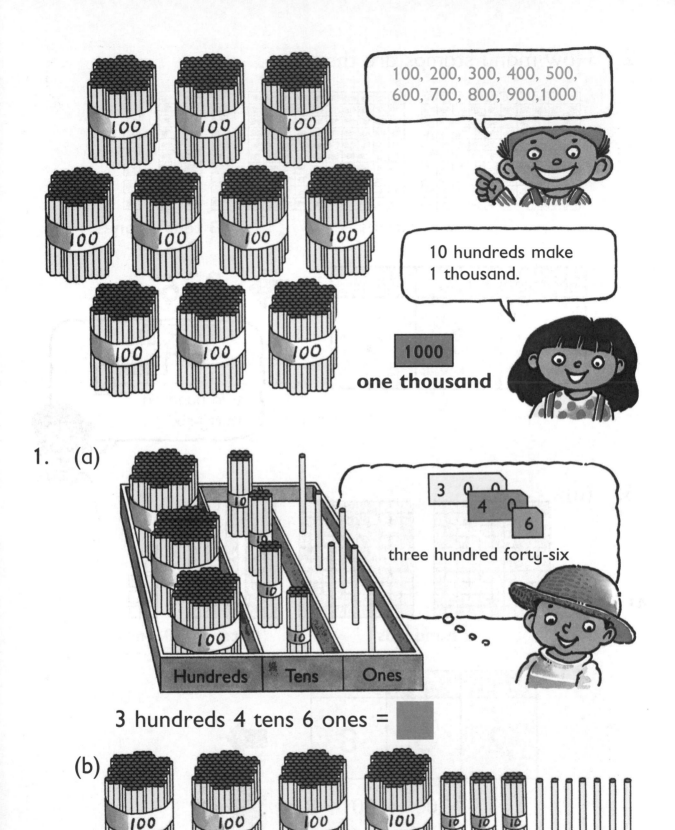

100, 200, 300, 400, 500, 600, 700, 800, 900, 1000

10 hundreds make 1 thousand.

1000

one thousand

1. (a)

three hundred forty-six

Hundreds | Tens | Ones

3 hundreds 4 tens 6 ones =

(b)

hundreds tens ones =

15

2. How many stamps are there?

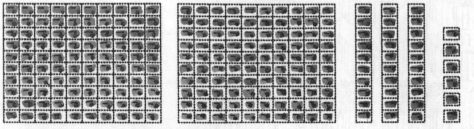

2 hundreds   **3 tens**   **6 ones**

Hundreds	Tens	Ones
2	3	6

➡ 236

two hundred thirty-six

3. (a)

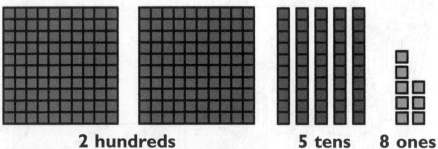

2 hundreds   **5 tens**   **8 ones**

Hundreds	Tens	Ones
2	5	8

➡

200 + 50 + 8 = ▢

(b) 400 + 70 = ▢   (c) 800 + 9 = ▢

4. This is a one-hundred-dollar bill.

one hundred dollars

(a)

$460

four hundred sixty dollars

(b)

$604

six hundred four dollars

(c) How many ten-dollar bills can we change for a one-hundred-dollar bill?

5. This is a one-thousand-dollar bill.

one thousand dollars

How many one-hundred-dollar bills can we change for a one-thousand-dollar bill?

6.

10 = 1 1 1 1 1 1 1 1 1 1

100 = 10 10 10 10 10 10 10 10 10 10

1000 = 100 100 100 100 100 100 100 100 100 100

(a) How many 1 can we change for a 100 ?

(b) How many 1 can we change for a 1000 ?

7. This chart shows 623.

Hundreds	Tens	Ones
100 100 100 100 100 100	10 10	1 1 1

623 = ▢ hundreds ▢ tens ▢ ones

8. What number does each chart show?

(a)

Hundreds	Tens	Ones
100 100 100 100	10 10 10 10 10 10	1 1 1 1 1 1 1

(b)

Hundreds	Tens	Ones
100 100	10 10 10 10 10	

(c)

Hundreds	Tens	Ones
100 100 100		1 1 1 1 1 1

19

9. (a) What number is 1 more than 253?

Hundreds	Tens	Ones

(b) What number is 10 more than 123?

Hundreds	Tens	Ones

(c) What number is 100 less than 341?

Hundreds	Tens	Ones

10. (a) What number is 1 more than 799?

(b) What number is 10 less than 500?

(c) What number is 100 more than 470?

20

PRACTICE 1B

1. Write the numbers in words.
   (a) 330   (b) 144   (c) 255   (d) 608

2. Write the numbers in hundreds, tens and ones.
   (a) 645   (b) 720   (c) 409   (d) 900

3. Write the numbers.
   (a) seven hundred four
   (b) five hundred forty
   (c) 3 hundreds 4 ones
   (d) 8 hundreds 2 tens

4. Which sign would you use, > or <?
   (a) 439 ● 426   (b) 290 ● 300
   (c) 506 ● 56   (d) 620 ● 602

5. Arrange the numbers in order.
   Begin with the smallest.
   (a) 99, 609, 410
   (b) 410, 140, 401, 104

6. (a) What number is 1 more than 299?
   (b) What number is 1 less than 780?

7. (a) What number is 10 more than 462?
   (b) What number is 10 less than 800?

8. (a) What number is 100 more than 599?
   (b) What number is 100 less than 605?

2 Addition and Subtraction

1 Meanings of Addition and Subtraction

Ali has 8 toy cars.
David has 6 toy cars.
How many toy cars do they have altogether?

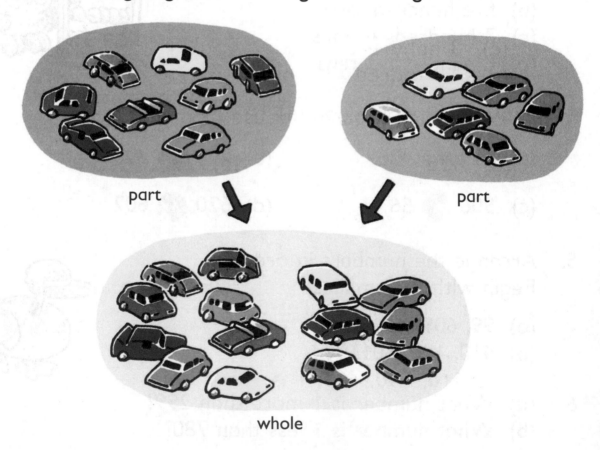

part

part

whole

$8 + 6 = \boxed{}$

They have $\boxed{}$ toy cars altogether.

1. Ali and David have **14** toy cars altogether.
   Ali has **8** toy cars.
   How many toy cars does David have?

$$14 - 8 = \boxed{}$$

To find the whole, we add.

To find one part, we subtract.

David has $\boxed{}$ toy cars.

2.

$$7 + 5 = \boxed{} \qquad\qquad 5 + 7 = \boxed{}$$

$$12 - 5 = \boxed{} \qquad\qquad 12 - 7 = \boxed{}$$

3.

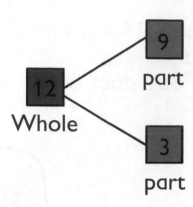

9 + 3 = ▢   3 + 9 = ▢

12 − 3 = ▢   12 − 9 = ▢

Workbook Exercise 8

4.

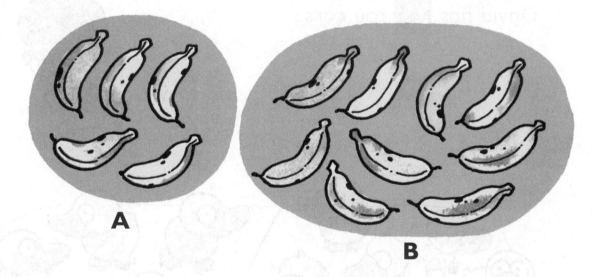

A

B

(a) How many more bananas are there in Set B than in Set A?

(b) 9 − 5 = ▢.

5. (a) 14 − 8 = ▢.

(b) 8 less than 14 is ▢.

Workbook Exercise 9

6. Add 21 and 35.

Tens	Ones
10 10 10 10 10	1 1 1 1 1 1

$$21 + 35 = \boxed{}$$

7. Subtract 13 from 27.

Tens	Ones
10 ~~10~~	1 1 1 1 ~~1~~ ~~1~~ ~~1~~

$$27 - 13 = \boxed{}$$

8.

$$32 + 13 = \boxed{} \qquad 45 - 13 = \boxed{}$$

$$13 + 32 = \boxed{} \qquad 45 - 32 = \boxed{}$$

9. Danny has **34** key chains.
   He buys **5** more.
   How many key chains does he have now?

$34 + 5 = \boxed{}$

Tens	Ones
10 10 10	1 1 1 1 1 1 1 1 1

Danny has $\boxed{}$ key chains now.

10. There are **24** green apples and **32** red apples.
    How many apples are there altogether?

$24 + 32 = \boxed{}$

Tens	Ones
10 10 10 10 10	1 1 1 1 1 1

There are $\boxed{}$ apples altogether.

26

11. Michael had **78** goldfish.
He sold **40** of them.
How many goldfish did he have left?

$$78 - 40 = \boxed{}$$

Tens	Ones
⑩ ⑩ ⑩ ⑩̶ ⑩̶ ⑩̶ ⑩̶	① ① ① ① ① ① ① ①

He had $\boxed{}$ goldfish left.

12. Rahmat has **48** stickers.
Samy has **32** stickers.
How many more stickers does Rahmat have than Samy?

$$48 - 32 = \boxed{}$$

Tens	Ones
⑩ ⑩ ⑩ ⑩ ⑩ ⑩ ⑩	① ① ① ① ① ① ① ① ① ①

Rahmat has $\boxed{}$ more stickers than Samy.

27

2 Addition Without Renaming

There are 236 boys and 362 girls.
How many children are there?

$$236 + 362 = \boxed{}$$

There are $\boxed{}$ children.

We can add like this:

H	T	O
2	3	6
+ 3	6	2
5	9	8

Hundreds	Tens	Ones

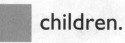

Add the ones.
6 ones + 2 ones
= 8 ones

Add the tens.
3 tens + 6 tens = 9 tens

Add the hundreds.
2 hundreds + 3 hundreds = 5 hundreds

$$\begin{array}{r} 2\,3\,6 \\ +\ 3\,6\,2 \\ \hline 8 \end{array}$$

$$\begin{array}{r} 2\,3\,6 \\ +\ 3\,6\,2 \\ \hline 9\,8 \end{array}$$

$$\begin{array}{r} 2\,3\,6 \\ +\ 3\,6\,2 \\ \hline 5\,9\,8 \end{array}$$

28

1. (a) $2 + 3 = $ ▢

   (b) $20 + 30 = $ ▢

   (c) $200 + 300 = $ ▢

2. Add 25 and 32.

$$\begin{array}{r} 25 \\ + \ \ 32 \\ \hline \end{array}$$

Tens	Ones
⑩ ⑩ ⑩ ⑩ ⑩	① ① ① ① ① ① ①

3. Find the value of

   (a) $61 + 8$ (b) $75 + 4$ (c) $34 + 24$

   (d) $19 + 50$ (e) $60 + 34$ (f) $70 + 29$

Workbook Exercise 11

4. Add 251 and 34.

$$\begin{array}{r} 2\ 5\ 1 \\ + \ \ \ \ 3\ 4 \\ \hline \end{array}$$

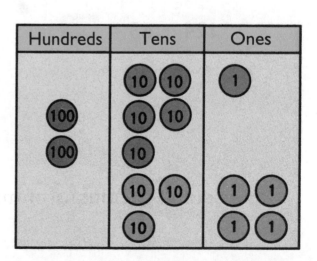

Hundreds	Tens	Ones
⑩⑩	⑩ ⑩ ⑩ ⑩ ⑩ ⑩ ⑩ ⑩	① ① ① ① ①

5. Add 245 and 142.

$$\begin{array}{r} 2\ 4\ 5 \\ +\ 1\ 4\ 2 \\ \hline \end{array}$$

Hundreds	Tens	Ones

6. Find the value of

(a) 104 + 30 (b) 230 + 60 (c) 125 + 72
(d) 539 + 50 (e) 442 + 134 (f) 342 + 253

7. Mr. Lin sold 124 cartons of milk on Saturday.
He sold 65 cartons of milk on Sunday.
How many cartons of milk did he sell altogether?

124 + 65 = ▮

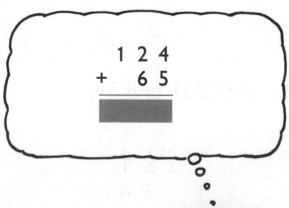

$$\begin{array}{r} 1\ 2\ 4 \\ +\ \ \ 6\ 5 \\ \hline \end{array}$$

He sold ▮ cartons of milk altogether.

30

3 Subtraction Without Renaming

There are **396** children.
214 of them are boys.
How many girls are there?

$$396 - 214 = \boxed{}$$

There are $\boxed{}$ girls.

We can subtract like this:

H	T	O
3	9	6
− 2	1	4
1	8	2

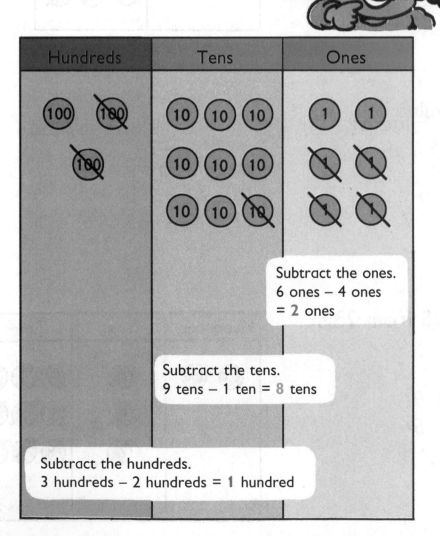

Hundreds	Tens	Ones

Subtract the ones.
6 ones − 4 ones
= **2** ones

Subtract the tens.
9 tens − 1 ten = **8** tens

Subtract the hundreds.
3 hundreds − 2 hundreds = **1** hundred

$$\begin{array}{r} 3\,9\,6 \\ -\,2\,1\,4 \\ \hline 2 \end{array}$$

$$\begin{array}{r} 3\,9\,6 \\ -\,2\,1\,4 \\ \hline 8\,2 \end{array}$$

$$\begin{array}{r} 3\,9\,6 \\ -\,2\,1\,4 \\ \hline 1\,8\,2 \end{array}$$

31

1. (a) $7 - 3$ = ⬜

   (b) $70 - 30$ = ⬜

   (c) $700 - 300$ = ⬜

2. Subtract 12 from 36.

$$\begin{array}{r} 3\ 6 \\ -\ 1\ 2 \\ \hline \end{array}$$

Tens	Ones
10 10 10̸	1 1 1 1 1̸ 1̸

3. Find the value of

   (a) $78 - 4$ (b) $78 - 40$
   (c) $65 - 5$ (d) $65 - 50$
   (e) $59 - 37$ (f) $48 - 38$

Workbook Exercise 13

4. Subtract 25 from 239.

$$\begin{array}{r} 2\ 3\ 9 \\ -\ \ \ 2\ 5 \\ \hline \end{array}$$

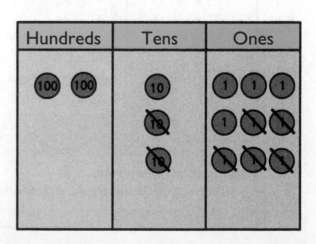

Hundreds	Tens	Ones
100 100	10 10̸ 10̸	1 1 1 1 1̸ 1̸ 1̸ 1̸ 1̸

5. Subtract 152 from 376.

Hundreds	Tens	Ones

$$\begin{array}{r} 3\ 7\ 6 \\ -\ 1\ 5\ 2 \\ \hline \end{array}$$

6. Find the value of

   (a) $486 - 80$ (b) $178 - 100$
   (c) $597 - 85$ (d) $269 - 62$
   (e) $365 - 145$ (f) $486 - 160$

7. There were 287 people in a hall.
   52 of them were children.
   How many adults were there?

   $287 - 52 = $ ▢

$$\begin{array}{r} 2\ 8\ 7 \\ -\ \ \ 5\ 2 \\ \hline \end{array}$$

   There were ▢ adults.

PRACTICE 2A

Find the value of each of the following:

	(a)	(b)	(c)
1.	34 + 3	56 + 20	61 + 27
2.	65 − 4	79 − 40	86 − 35
3.	42 + 35	97 + 2	58 + 40
4.	64 − 44	67 − 31	45 − 23
5.	72 + 17	49 − 9	35 − 30

6. Devi had 36 stamps.
   She gave 11 of them away.
   How many stamps did she have left?

7. Mr. Stone bought 43 sticks of
   chicken satay and 24 sticks of
   beef satay.
   How many sticks of satay did he buy?

8. There are 48 cherries and 25 kiwis.
   How many more cherries than kiwis are there?

9. Mr. Gray sold 23 cans of drinks in the morning.
   He sold 76 cans of drinks in the afternoon.
   How many cans of drinks did he sell altogether?

10. Marisol wants to buy this book.
    She has only $14.
    How much more money does
    she need?

PRACTICE 2B

Find the value of each of the following:

	(a)	(b)	(c)
1.	354 + 5	147 + 21	253 + 346
2.	865 − 3	694 − 72	484 − 43
3.	163 + 30	267 + 300	185 + 412
4.	588 − 60	794 − 500	385 − 161
5.	364 + 124	856 − 354	697 − 90

6. After selling 245 buns, Mrs. Bates had 54 buns left. How many buns did she have at first?

7. In a class library, there are 568 English books and 204 Spanish books.
   How many more English books than Spanish books are there?

8. Maria had 439 eggs.
   She sold 326 of them.
   How many eggs had she left?

9. 768 people were at a football game.
   532 of them were adults.
   How many of them were children?

10. 104 boys and 125 girls took part in a swimming test.

   (a) How many children took part in the test?
   (b) How many more girls than boys were there?

4 **Addition With Renaming**

Add 36 and 28.

When there are 10 ones or more, change 10 ones for 1 ten.

$$\begin{array}{r} 3\ 6 \\ +\ 2\ 8 \\ \hline \end{array}$$

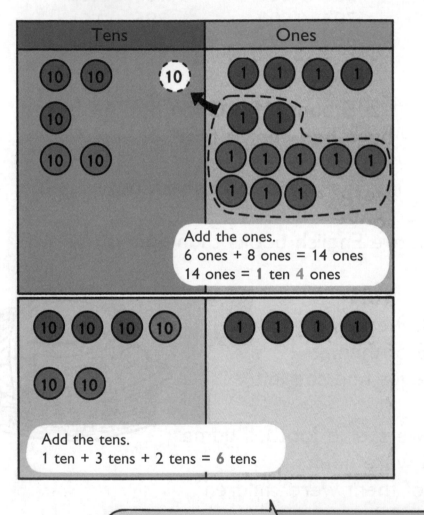

Tens	Ones

Add the ones.
6 ones + 8 ones = 14 ones
14 ones = **1** ten **4** ones

Add the tens.
1 ten + 3 tens + 2 tens = **6** tens

$$\begin{array}{r} ^1 \\ 3\ 6 \\ +\ 2\ 8 \\ \hline 4 \end{array}$$

$$\begin{array}{r} ^1 \\ 3\ 6 \\ +\ 2\ 8 \\ \hline 6\ 4 \end{array}$$

$$\begin{array}{r} ^1 \\ 3\ 6 \\ +\ 2\ 8 \\ \hline 4 \end{array}$$

Add the ones.

$$\begin{array}{r} ^1 \\ 3\ 6 \\ +\ 2\ 8 \\ \hline 6\ 4 \end{array}$$

Add the tens.

36

1. Find the value of

   (a) $4 + 9$ (b) $60 + 9$
   (c) $64 + 9$ (d) $40 + 90$
   (e) $600 + 9$ (f) $640 + 90$

2. Find the value of

   (a) $35 + 7$ (b) $75 + 5$
   (c) $48 + 38$ (d) $54 + 29$
   (e) $57 + 13$ (f) $69 + 31$

Workbook Exercise 15

3. Add 318 and 43.

$$\begin{array}{r} 3\ 1\ 8 \\ +\ \ \ 4\ 3 \\ \hline \end{array}$$

Hundreds	Tens	Ones

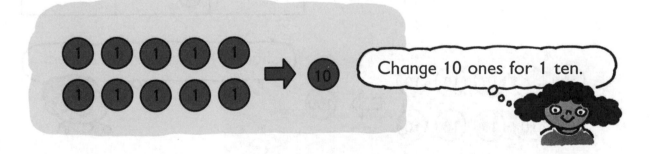

Change 10 ones for 1 ten.

4. Find the value of

   (a) $315 + 8$ (b) $224 + 7$
   (c) $527 + 45$ (d) $608 + 48$
   (e) $734 + 36$ (f) $321 + 69$

37

5. Add 267 and 123.

$$\begin{array}{r} 2\ 6\ 7 \\ +\ 1\ 2\ 3 \\ \hline \end{array}$$

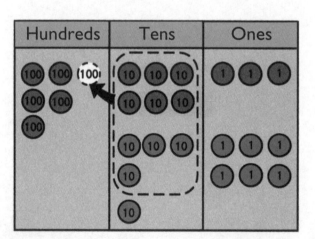

6. Find the value of

   (a) 127 + 365   (b) 452 + 219   (c) 639 + 124
   (d) 745 + 136   (e) 506 + 104   (f) 828 + 162

7. Add 563 and 56.

$$\begin{array}{r} 5\ 6\ 3 \\ +\ \ \ 5\ 6 \\ \hline \end{array}$$

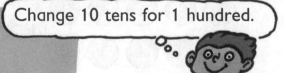

Change 10 tens for 1 hundred.

8. Find the value of

   (a) 292 + 60   (b) 574 + 70   (c) 385 + 63
   (d) 630 + 94   (e) 420 + 80   (f) 279 + 30

38

9. Add 382 and 145.

$$\begin{array}{r} 3\ 8\ 2 \\ +\ 1\ 4\ 5 \\ \hline \end{array}$$

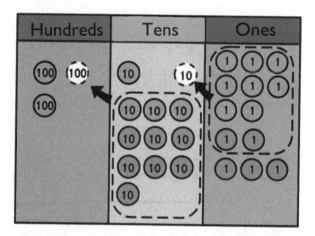

Hundreds	Tens	Ones
(100) (100)	(10)(10)(10)	(1)(1)
(100)	(10)(10)(10)	
(100)	(10)(10)	
(100)	(10)(10)	(1)(1)(1)
	(10)(10)	(1)(1)

10. Find the value of

(a) 454 + 163   (b) 670 + 156
(c) 257 + 351   (d) 588 + 220
(e) 363 + 255   (f) 790 + 139

Workbook Exercises 16 & 17

11. Add 248 and 75.

$$\begin{array}{r} 2\ 4\ 8 \\ +\ \ \ 7\ 5 \\ \hline \end{array}$$

Hundreds	Tens	Ones
(100) (100)	(10) (10)	(1)(1)(1)
(100)	(10)(10)(10)	(1)(1)(1)
	(10)(10)(10)	(1)(1)
	(10)(10)(10)	(1)(1)
	(10)	(1)(1)(1)

$$\begin{array}{r} \overset{1}{}\ \ \\ 2\ 4\ 8 \\ +\ \ \ 7\ 5 \\ \hline 3 \end{array}$$
Add the ones.

$$\begin{array}{r} \overset{1}{}\overset{1}{}\ \\ 2\ 4\ 8 \\ +\ \ \ 7\ 5 \\ \hline 2\ 3 \end{array}$$
Add the tens.

$$\begin{array}{r} \overset{1}{}\overset{1}{}\ \\ 2\ 4\ 8 \\ +\ \ \ 7\ 5 \\ \hline 3\ 2\ 3 \end{array}$$
Add the hundreds.

39

12. Find the value of

    (a) 265 + 69   (b) 493 + 28   (c) 684 + 19

13. Add 237 and 184.

    $\begin{array}{r} 2\ 3\ 7 \\ +\ 1\ 8\ 4 \\ \hline \end{array}$

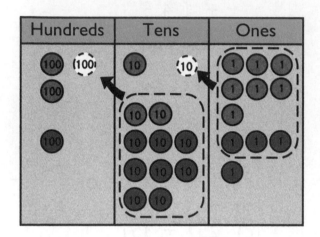

14. Find the value of

    (a) 178 + 443   (b) 204 + 398   (c) 465 + 135

15. Add 186, 249 and 38.

    $\begin{array}{r} 1\ 8\ 6 \\ 2\ 4\ 9 \\ +\quad 3\ 8 \\ \hline \end{array}$

We add 3 numbers in the same way.

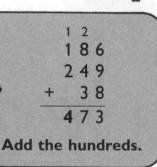

$\begin{array}{r}2\ \ \ \\ 1\ 8\ 6\\ 2\ 4\ 9\\ +\quad 3\ 8\\ \hline 3\end{array}$	$\begin{array}{r}1\ 2\ \\ 1\ 8\ 6\\ 2\ 4\ 9\\ +\quad 3\ 8\\ \hline 7\ 3\end{array}$	$\begin{array}{r}1\ 2\ \\ 1\ 8\ 6\\ 2\ 4\ 9\\ +\quad 3\ 8\\ \hline 4\ 7\ 3\end{array}$
Add the ones.	**Add the tens.**	**Add the hundreds.**

16. Find the value of

    (a) 172 + 487 + 74   (b) 209 + 145 + 567

40

PRACTICE 2C

Find the value of each of the following:

	(a)	(b)	(c)
1.	$26 + 9$	$32 + 8$	$46 + 7$
2.	$35 + 28$	$51 + 29$	$63 + 27$
3.	$44 + 56$	$58 + 42$	$74 + 26$
4.	$27 + 80$	$33 + 82$	$49 + 70$
5.	$53 + 62$	$64 + 65$	$72 + 37$

6. Brian has 92 Singapore stamps and 42 Malaysian stamps.
   How many more Singapore stamps than Malaysian stamps does he have?

7. After selling 86 sticks of satay, Mrs. Aminah had 22 sticks of satay left.
   How many sticks of satay did she have at first?

8. Samy bought 58 greeting cards.
   He used 42 of them.
   How many cards did he have left?

9. Lily is 18 years old.
   Her father is 26 years older than she.
   How old is her father?

10. Juan sold 46 cream puffs in the morning.
    He sold another 28 in the afternoon.
    He still had 16 cream puffs left.
    (a) How many cream puffs did he sell?
    (b) How many cream puffs did he have at first?

41

PRACTICE 2D

Find the value of each of the following:

	(a)	(b)	(c)
1.	264 + 50	379 + 60	342 + 93
2.	407 + 38	532 + 48	644 + 49
3.	745 + 108	829 + 122	667 + 227
4.	490 + 139	584 + 250	876 + 19
5.	293 + 60 + 24	339 + 104 + 40	224 + 106 + 320

6. Weili has 169 stamps.
   His friend gives him 71 more.
   How many stamps does he have now?

7. A tailor bought 240 white
   buttons and 85 black buttons.
   How many buttons did he
   buy altogether?

8. There were 102 boys, 86 girls and 40 adults at a
   concert.
   How many people were there at the concert?

9. Justin made 285 pizzas.
   He sold some of them and had 70 pizzas left.
   How many pizzas did he sell?

10. Devi saved $125.
    Samy saved $36 more than Devi.
    How much did Samy save?

42

5 Subtraction With Renaming

Subtract 43 from 62.

$$\begin{array}{r} 6\ 2 \\ -\ \ 4\ 3 \\ \hline \end{array}$$

When there are not enough ones to subtract from, change 1 ten for 10 ones.

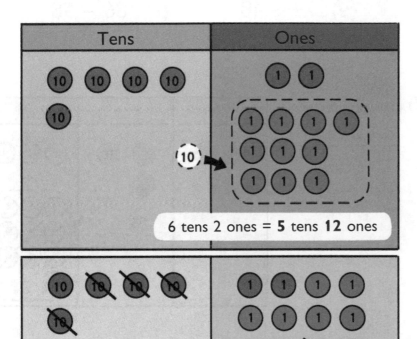

Tens	Ones

6 tens 2 ones = **5** tens **12** ones

Subtract the tens.
5 tens − 4 tens = **1** ten

Subtract the ones.
12 ones − 3 ones
= **9** ones

$$\begin{array}{r} \overset{5\ \ 12}{6\ \ 2} \\ -\ \ 4\ 3 \\ \hline \end{array}$$

$$\begin{array}{r} \overset{5\ \ 12}{6\ \ 2} \\ -\ \ 4\ 3 \\ \hline 9 \end{array}$$

$$\begin{array}{r} \overset{5\ \ 12}{6\ \ 2} \\ -\ \ 4\ 3 \\ \hline 1\ 9 \end{array}$$

$$\begin{array}{r} \overset{5\ \ 12}{6\ \ 2} \\ -\ \ 4\ 3 \\ \hline 9 \end{array}$$
Subtract the ones.

$$\begin{array}{r} \overset{5\ \ 12}{6\ \ 2} \\ -\ \ 4\ 3 \\ \hline 1\ 9 \end{array}$$
Subtract the tens.

43

1. Find the value of each of the following:
   (a) 10 − 6   (b) 11 − 6   (c)   41 − 6
   (d) 100 − 60   (e) 110 − 60   (f) 410 − 60

2. Find the value of
   (a) 30 − 6   (b) 41 − 9   (c) 52 − 13
   (d) 63 − 35   (e) 74 − 48   (f) 86 − 58

3. Subtract 18 from 243.

   $$\begin{array}{r} 2\,4\,3 \\ -\ \ 1\,8 \\ \hline \end{array}$$

Hundreds	Tens	Ones

Change 1 ten for 10 ones.

4. Find the value of
   (a) 354 − 9   (b) 480 − 7   (c) 562 − 34
   (d) 690 − 45   (e) 720 − 18   (f) 833 − 29

5. Subtract 134 from 452.

$$\begin{array}{r} 4\ 5\ 2 \\ -\ 1\ 3\ 4 \\ \hline \end{array}$$

Hundreds	Tens	Ones

6. Find the value of

(a) 441 – 227   (b) 553 – 228   (c) 764 – 506
(d) 470 – 256   (e) 625 – 118   (f) 830 – 724

7. Subtract 64 from 729.

$$\begin{array}{r} 7\ 2\ 9 \\ -\ \ \ 6\ 4 \\ \hline \end{array}$$

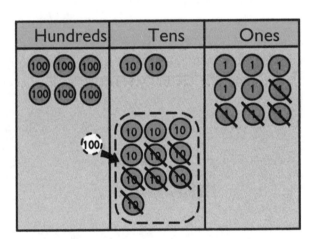

Change 1 hundred for 10 tens.

8. Find the value of

(a) 348 – 76   (b) 409 – 38   (c) 516 – 54
(d) 707 – 61   (e) 620 – 80   (f) 139 – 83

45

9. Subtract 293 from 538.

$$
\begin{array}{r}
5\ 3\ 8 \\
-\ 2\ 9\ 3 \\
\hline
\end{array}
$$

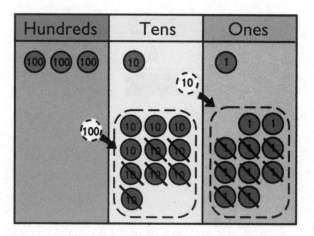

Hundreds	Tens	Ones

10. Find the value of

(a) $617 - 247$ (b) $308 - 140$
(c) $705 - 492$ (d) $807 - 486$
(e) $634 - 284$ (f) $920 - 840$

Workbook Exercises 20 & 21

11. Subtract 68 from 421.

$$
\begin{array}{r}
4\ 2\ 1 \\
-\ \ \ 6\ 8 \\
\hline
\end{array}
$$

Hundreds	Tens	Ones

$$
\begin{array}{r}
{}^{1}\ {}^{11} \\
4\ 2\!\!\!/\ 1\!\!\!/ \\
-\ \ \ 6\ 8 \\
\hline
3
\end{array}
$$

Subtract the ones.

$$
\begin{array}{r}
3\ \ 1\ {}^{11} \\
4\!\!\!/\ 2\!\!\!/\ 1\!\!\!/ \\
-\ \ \ 6\ 8 \\
\hline
5\ 3
\end{array}
$$

Subtract the tens.

$$
\begin{array}{r}
3\ \ 11\ 11 \\
4\!\!\!/\ 2\!\!\!/\ 1\!\!\!/ \\
-\ \ \ 6\ 8 \\
\hline
3\ 5\ 3
\end{array}
$$

Subtract the hundreds.

46

12. Find the value of

    (a) 322 − 47   (b) 430 − 55   (c) 631 − 78

13. Subtract 267 from 453.

```
    4 5 3
  − 2 6 7
  ─────────
```

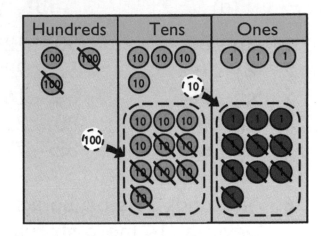

14. Find the value of

    (a) 512 − 149   (b) 640 − 276   (c) 623 − 246

Workbook Exercise 22

15. Subtract 28 from 300.

```
     2 9 10
     3̶ 0̶ 0̶
  −     2 8
  ─────────
```

Change 1 hundred for 9 tens and 10 ones.

16. Find the value of

    (a) 400 − 38   (b) 700 − 276   (c) 402 − 337

Workbook Exercises 23 & 24

PRACTICE 2E

Find the value of each of the following:

	(a)	(b)	(c)
1.	40 − 8	50 − 12	60 − 24
2.	41 − 14	52 − 23	63 − 38
3.	53 − 35	64 − 16	74 − 29
4.	70 − 61	80 − 73	90 − 89
5.	73 − 68	82 − 77	91 − 86

6. Ailian has 18 storybooks.
   Devi has 14 more storybooks than Ailian.
   How many storybooks does Devi have?

7. Jenny collected 92 shells.
   She collected 9 more shells than Mary.
   How many shells did Mary collect?

8. Sara bought 84 T-shirts.
   She gave 15 of them to her friends.
   How many T-shirts did she have left?

9. Mrs. Cohen went shopping with $92.
   She spent $58.
   How much money did she have left?

10. Holly bought this dictionary.
    She still had $28 left.
    How much money did she
    have at first?

48

PRACTICE 2F

Find the value of each of the following:

	(a)	(b)	(c)
1.	400 − 80	502 − 70	630 − 90
2.	100 − 23	400 − 92	503 − 78
3.	290 − 128	370 − 163	460 − 253
4.	530 − 139	642 − 248	753 − 359
5.	600 − 423	703 − 287	904 − 827

6. There are 320 chairs in a hall.
   180 of them are new.
   How many chairs are **not** new?

7. There are 224 red buttons and 298 yellow buttons.
   How many buttons are there altogether?

8. Samy had 105 picture cards.
   After giving some away, he had
   87 picture cards left.
   How many picture cards did he give away?

9. Lihua needs 620 beads to make a bag.
   She has only 465 beads.
   How many more beads does she need?

10. There are 304 girls in a school.
    There are 46 fewer boys than girls.
    (a) How many boys are there in the school?
    (b) How many children are there in the school?

PRACTICE 2G

Find the value of each of the following:

	(a)	(b)	(c)
1.	40 + 39	52 + 27	61 + 38
2.	79 − 20	82 − 42	96 − 90
3.	70 + 38	64 + 16	32 + 77
4.	80 − 47	71 − 36	92 − 87
5.	66 + 34	79 + 22	88 + 19

6. Sally and Kelly have 98 postcards altogether.
   Sally has 39 postcards.
   How many postcards does Kelly have?

7. A farmer has 82 chickens.
   He has 24 more ducks than chickens.
   How many ducks does he have?

8. The table shows the result of a basketball game
   between two teams.

Team A	79 points
Team B	95 points

   Which team scored more points?
   How many more points did the
   winning team score?

9. David is 26 years old.
   Paul is 9 years older than David.
   Mary is 8 years older than Paul.
   (a) How old is Paul?
   (b) How old is Mary?

50

PRACTICE 2H

Find the value of each of the following:

	(a)	(b)	(c)
1.	$262 - 52$	$473 - 60$	$560 - 240$
2.	$122 + 77$	$236 + 52$	$340 + 359$
3.	$350 - 49$	$408 - 148$	$607 - 560$
4.	$247 + 37$	$375 + 180$	$408 + 199$
5.	$500 - 142$	$603 - 266$	$710 - 614$

6. There are 427 cars in Parking Lot A.
   There are 278 cars in Parking Lot B.
   How many cars are there in the two parking lots?

7. There are 152 desks in a hall.
   There are 35 fewer chairs than desks.
   How many chairs are there in the hall?

8. Angela had $220.
   After buying a watch, she had $186 left.
   How much did the watch cost?

9. 140 children took part in a swimming test.
   23 of them failed the test.
   How many children passed the test?

10. The total cost of a calculator and a watch is $212.
    The watch costs $144.
    (a) Find the cost of the calculator.
    (b) Which costs more, the watch
        or the calculator?
        How much more?

3

Length

1 **Measuring Length in Meters**

Ali　　　　Ben

Who is taller than 1 meter?
Who is shorter than 1 meter?

Measure your height with a meter rule.
Are you taller than 1 meter or shorter than 1 meter?

1. Measure your teacher's desk with a meter rule.

The length of the desk is more than 1 meter.

Its width is about 1 meter.

2. Cut a string 1 meter long.
   Use it to measure the length of the chalkboard in your classroom.

The **meter** is a unit of length.
We write **m** for meter.

Is the length of the chalkboard more than 3 m or less than 3 m?

53

Workbook Exercise 25

3.

The red ribbon is 7 m long.
The blue ribbon is 4 m long.
(a) What is the total length of the two ribbons?
(b) How much longer is the red ribbon than the blue ribbon?

4.

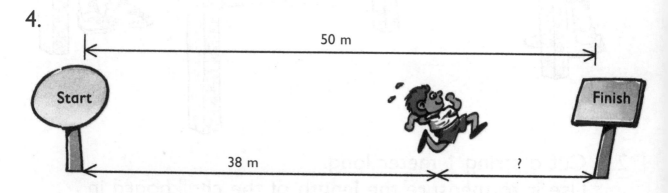

Paul is running in a 50-meter race.
He is 38 m from the starting point.
How many meters is he from the finishing point?

5. Mrs. Wu bought 60 m of cloth.
After making some curtains, she had 24 m of cloth left.
How many meters of cloth did she use?

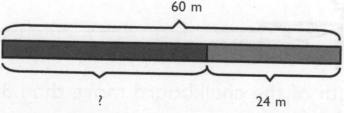

2 Measuring Length in Centimeters

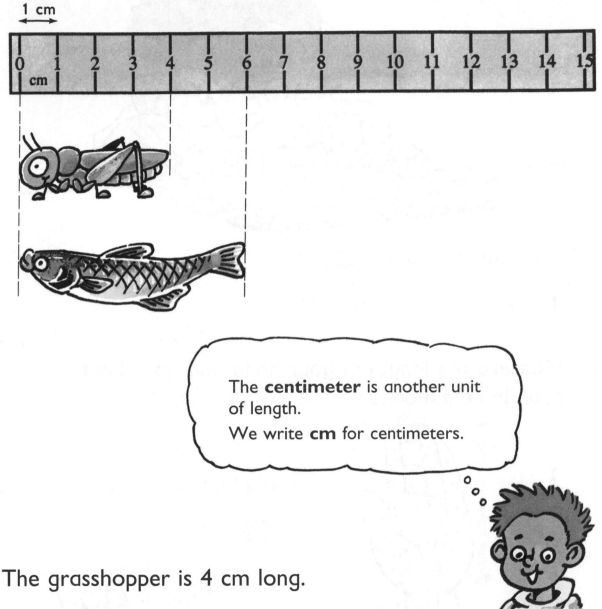

The **centimeter** is another unit of length.
We write **cm** for centimeters.

The grasshopper is 4 cm long.

The fish is 6 cm long.

The grasshopper is ▢ cm shorter than the fish.

The fish is ▢ cm longer than the grasshopper.

55

1. Use your ruler to measure the length and width of your textbook.

The length is about ▮ cm.

The width is about ▮ cm.

2. Measure the length of your hand and your hand span in centimeters.

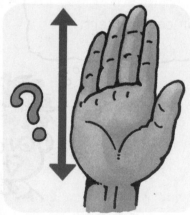

My hand is about

▮ cm long.

My hand span is about

▮ cm long.

Which is longer, your hand or your hand span? How much longer?

56

3. Cut a piece of string as long as the line.
   Then measure the length of the string with your ruler.

4. Measure these lines.

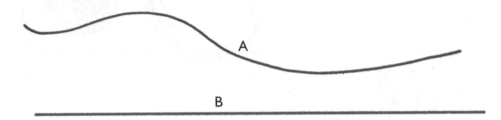

A

B

Line A is about ☐ cm long.

Line B is about ☐ cm long.

Which line is longer?
How much longer?

5. Susan is going to the post office.
   Which is the shortest way?
   Which is the longest way?

6. Use a measuring tape to measure your waist in centimeters.

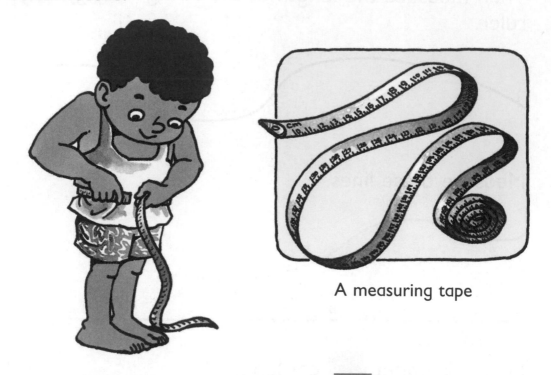

A measuring tape

The length of my waist is about ▮ cm.

Workbook Exercise 27

7. Use your ruler to draw a line **8 cm** long.

3 Measuring Length in Yards and Feet

We also measure length in yards and feet.

1. Measure your teacher's desk with a yard stick.

Is the length more than a yard?
Is the width more than a yard?

2. Measure your height with the yard stick.

Are you taller than 1 yard or shorter than 1 yard?

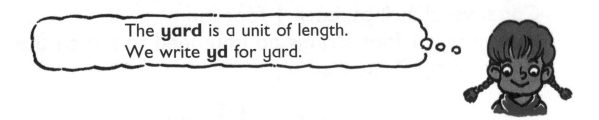

The **yard** is a unit of length.
We write **yd** for yard.

59

3. Cut a string 1 foot long.
    Use it to measure the length
    of your desk.

    Is the length of your desk more than
    1 foot or less than 1 foot?

    > The **foot** is a unit of length.
    > If we have more than one foot, we call them feet.
    > We write **ft** for foot or feet.

    We read 1 ft as 1 foot, and 2 ft as 2 feet.

4. Cut a string 1 foot long. Cut a string 1 yard long.
    Place the two strings side by side.

    String A   1 foot

    String B   1 yard

    Which string is longer?

    Cut several strings, each 1 foot long.
    How many 1-foot strings do you need to match the
    length of the 1-yard string?

    1 yard = ▢ feet

4 Measuring Length in Inches

We also measure length in inches.

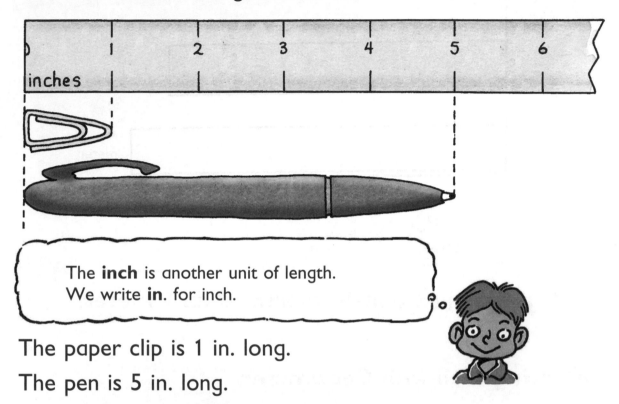

The **inch** is another unit of length.
We write **in.** for inch.

The paper clip is 1 in. long.

The pen is 5 in. long.

The paper clip is ⬛ in. shorter than the pen.

The pen is ⬛ in. longer than the paper clip.

Take a look at your ruler. How many inches are there in 1 foot?

1 foot = ⬛ **inches**

1. Use your ruler to measure the length and width of your textbook.

   The length is about ⬛ in.

   The width is about ⬛ in.

61

Comparing Yard with Meter

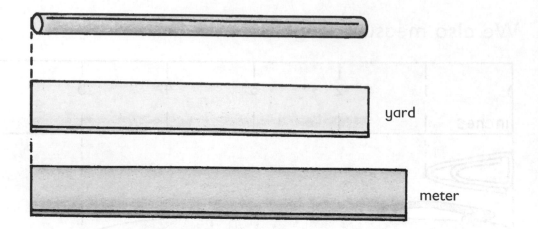

yard

meter

The rod is 1 yd long.
It is about 1 m long.

1 yard is just a little shorter than 1 meter.

Comparing Inch with Centimeter

Line A $\underline{\quad 1\ cm \quad}$

Line B $\underline{\qquad 1\ in. \qquad}$

Which line is longer?

1 inch is longer than 1 centimeter.

We use feet, yards and meters to measure longer objects.
We use inches and centimeters to measure shorter objects.

62

Workbook Exercise 28

PRACTICE 3A

Find the value of each of the following:

	(a)	(b)	(c)
1.	285 + 9	329 + 70	454 + 46
2.	262 + 309	374 + 128	675 + 285
3.	392 − 8	267 − 80	473 − 95
4.	337 − 208	400 − 196	503 − 184
5.	624 + 176	370 − 192	800 − 106

6.

Samy's house   350 m   550 m

Samy walked to the post office and then to the library.
How far did he walk?

7. Lily bought a piece of ribbon **90 cm** long.
She had **35 cm** of it left after making a bow.
How many centimeters of ribbon did she use to make the bow?

8. What is the total length around the field?

9. Taylor is **96 cm** tall.
Nicole is **8 cm** shorter than Taylor.
What is Nicole's height?

24 yd
16 yd   Field   12 yd
12 yd

63

4 Weight

1 Measuring Weight in Kilograms

The **kilogram** is a unit of weight.
We write **kg** for kilogram.

Hold a 1-kilogram weight
in your hand.
Feel how heavy it is.

The book weighs less than 1 kg.

The bag weighs more than 1 kg.

Look for an object which weighs about 1 kg.

1. Make a bag of beans which weighs 1 kg.

2. (a)

The prawns weigh ▢ kg.

(b)

The newspapers weigh ▢ kg.

65

3.

Is the papaya heavier than 1 kg or lighter than 1 kg?

4.

Is the weight of the durian more than 2 kg or less than 2 kg?

5. The weight of the bag is ⬛ kg.

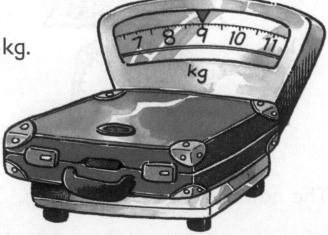

6.

(a) Which package is heavier?
    How much heavier?
(b) What is the total weight of the two packages?

7.

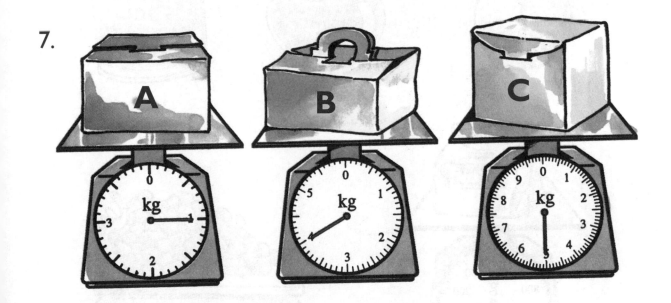

(a) Which package is the heaviest?
(b) Which package is the lightest?
(c) What is the total weight of the three packages?

67

Workbook Exercise 29

2 Measuring Weight in Grams

The **gram** is another unit of weight.
We write **g** for gram.

Find some of these objects and feel
how heavy they are.

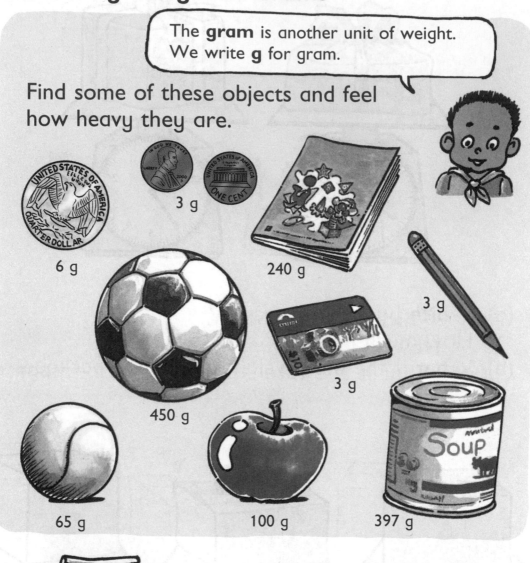

3 g

6 g

240 g

3 g

450 g

3 g

65 g

100 g

Soup

397 g

The flour weighs 650 g.

The grapes weigh 632 g.

68

1. (a)

The carrots weigh

 g.

(b)

The fish weighs

 g.

2. (a)

The mushrooms weigh g.

(b)

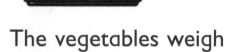

The vegetables weigh

g.

3. Measure the weight of these objects in grams.

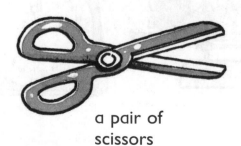

a pair of scissors

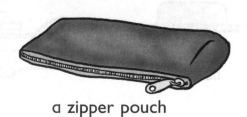

a zipper pouch

3 Measuring Weight in Pounds

We also measure weight in pounds.

The **pound** is a unit of weight.
We write **lb** for pound.

Hold a 1-pound weight in your hand.
Feel how heavy it is.

1. Make a bag of beans which weighs 1 lb.

70

2.

Is the watermelon heavier than 1 lb or lighter than 1 lb?

3.

(a) Which package is lighter?
How much lighter?

(b) What is the total weight of the two packages?

4. Find out your weight in pounds using a bathroom scale.

4 Measuring Weight in Ounces

We also measure weight in ounces.

The **ounce** is another unit of weight.
We write **oz** for ounce.

1.

The apple weighs
 oz.

The mushrooms weigh
 oz.

2. Find the weight of these objects using a kitchen scale.

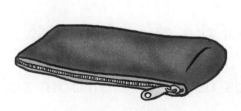

a zipper pouch

a mathematics book

Comparing Pound with Kilogram

Which is lighter?

1 pound is lighter than 1 kilogram.

Comparing Ounce with Gram

Which is heavier?

1 ounce is heavier than 1 gram.

PRACTICE 4A

Find the value of each of the following:

	(a)	(b)	(c)
1.	$253 + 8$	$368 + 40$	$476 + 57$
2.	$509 + 128$	$670 + 186$	$764 + 166$
3.	$202 - 9$	$357 - 70$	$402 - 82$
4.	$532 - 500$	$642 - 162$	$830 - 244$
5.	$843 - 289$	$267 + 356$	$804 - 269$

6. A durian weighs 900 g.
   A papaya weighs 550 g.
   (a) Which is heavier, the durian or the papaya?
   (b) How much heavier?

7. Raju weighs 39 kg.
   His father is 28 kg heavier than he.
   (a) Find the weight of Raju's father.
   (b) What is the total weight of Raju and his father?

8. A mango weighs 280 g.
   A pear is 60 g lighter than the mango.
   (a) What is the weight of the pear?
   (b) Find the total weight of the mango and
       the pear.

9. The total weight of an apple and a pineapple
   is 840 g.
   The apple weighs 90 g.
   (a) Find the weight of the pineapple.
   (b) How much heavier is the pineapple than the
       apple?

REVIEW A

Find the value of each of the following:

	(a)	(b)	(c)
1.	569 + 90	670 + 45	792 + 58
2.	327 + 650	296 + 364	465 + 535
3.	488 − 86	846 − 64	903 − 93
4.	743 − 243	622 − 272	520 − 488
5.	362 − 178	469 + 156	700 − 302

6. Samy bought 20 m of rope.
   He used 7 m of it to make a swing.
   How much rope was left?

7. Nicole used 96 cm of ribbon to tie a package.
   She used 85 cm of ribbon to tie another package.
   How many centimeters of ribbon did she use
   altogether?

8. The total weight of a papaya
   and a pear is 340 g.
   The pear weighs 95 g.
   What is the weight of the papaya?

9. Sulin weighs 34 kg.
   Her brother is 8 kg lighter than she.
   (a) What is the weight of her brother?
   (b) What is the total weight of Sulin and her brother?

75

5

Multiplication and Division

1 **Multiplication**

How many apples are there altogether?

$4 + 4 + 4 = 12$

3 groups of 4

$3 \times 4 = 12$

$4 \times 3 = 12$

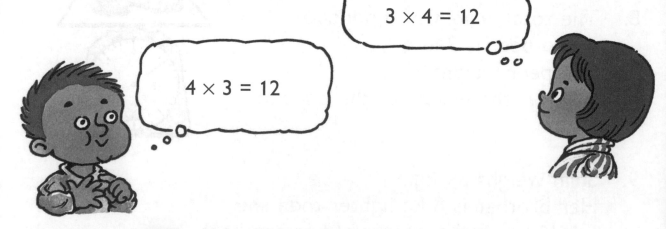

There are ▢ apples altogether.

76

This is **multiplication**.
We multiply to find the
total number.

1.

5×4

There are 5 birds in each nest.
There are ■ birds in 4 nests.

2.

5×6

There are 5 groups of 6.
There are ■ hats altogether.

77

3. (a) Multiply 7 by 3.

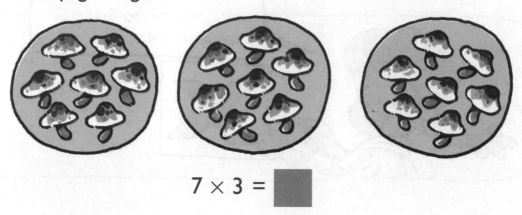

$7 \times 3 = $ ▢

(b) Multiply 9 by 4.

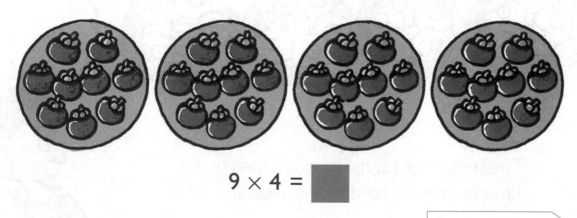

$9 \times 4 = $ ▢

Workbook Exercises 32 & 33

4. (a)

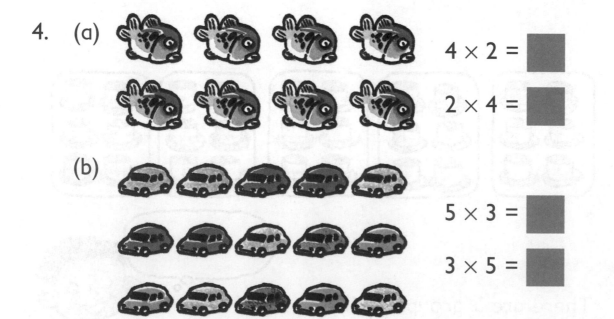

$4 \times 2 = $ ▢

$2 \times 4 = $ ▢

(b)

$5 \times 3 = $ ▢

$3 \times 5 = $ ▢

Workbook Exercise 34

PRACTICE 5A

1.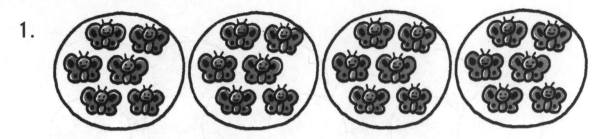

How many butterflies are there altogether?

2.

There are 2 buttons on each dress.
How many buttons are there on 5 dresses?

3. There are 6 chairs
in each row.
How many chairs are
there in 3 rows?

4. Jessica bought 3 boxes
of cakes.
There were 5 cakes in
each box.
How many cakes did she
buy altogether?

2 Division

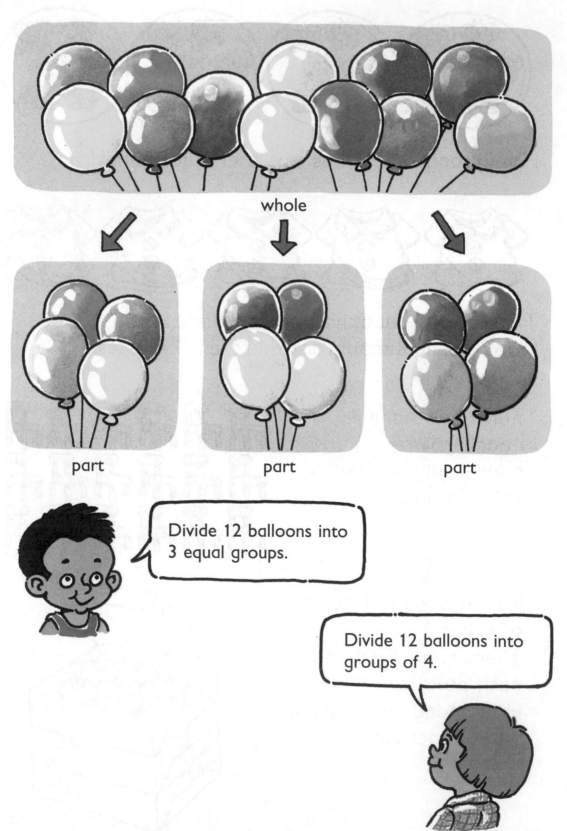

whole

part   part   part

Divide 12 balloons into 3 equal groups.

Divide 12 balloons into groups of 4.

80

1.

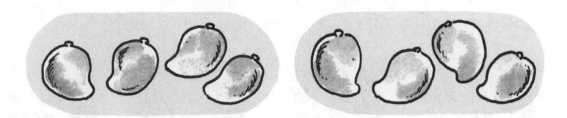

Divide 8 mangoes into 2 equal groups.
There are 4 mangoes in each group.

We write:

$$8 \div 2 = 4$$

Divide 8 by 2.
The answer is 4.

This is **division**.
We divide to find
the number in each
group.

2. Divide 20 boats into 4 equal groups.
   How many boats are there in each group?

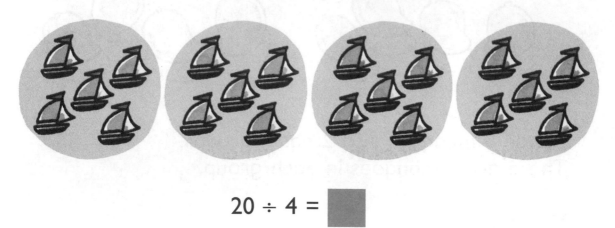

$$20 \div 4 = \boxed{}$$

There are $\boxed{}$ boats in each group.

3. Share 18 toy cars equally between 3 children.
   How many toy cars does each child get?

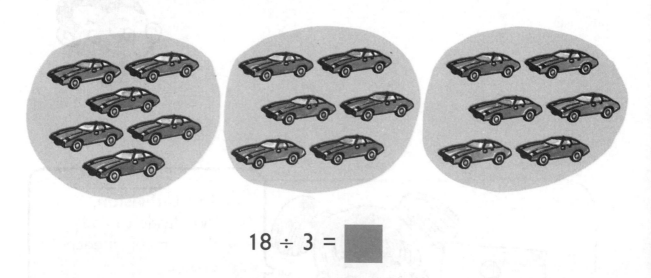

$$18 \div 3 = \boxed{}$$

Each child gets $\boxed{}$ toy cars.

Workbook Exercises 35 & 36

4.

Divide 15 children into groups of 5.
There are 3 groups.

We write:

$$15 \div 5 = 3$$

Divide 15 by 5.
The answer is 3.

We also divide to find
the number of groups.

5. Divide 30 shells into groups of 6.
   How many groups are there?

$$30 \div 6 = \boxed{}$$

There are $\boxed{}$ groups.

6. Lily uses 4 straws to make 1 square.
   How many squares can she make with 24 straws?

$$24 \div 4 = \boxed{}$$

She can make $\boxed{}$ squares.

84

7.

$9 \times 2 = \blacksquare$ $2 \times 9 = \blacksquare$

$18 \div 2 = \blacksquare$ $18 \div 9 = \blacksquare$

8.

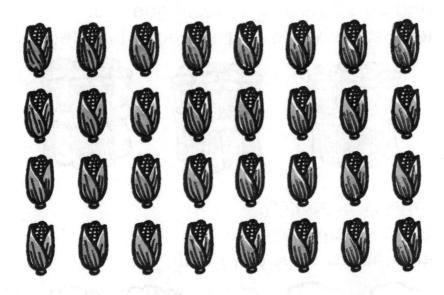

$8 \times 4 = \blacksquare$ $4 \times 8 = \blacksquare$

$32 \div 4 = \blacksquare$ $32 \div 8 = \blacksquare$

85

Workbook Exercise 39

PRACTICE 5B

1. Share 12 oranges equally between 2 children.
   How many oranges does each child get?

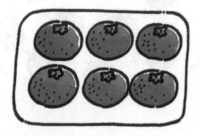

2. Pack 24 balls into boxes of 6.
   How many boxes are there?

3. Emma tied 30 sticks into 3 equal bundles.
   How many sticks were there in each bundle?

4. Lauren makes 28 cakes.
   She wants to put 4 cakes in each box.
   How many boxes does she need?

PRACTICE 5C

1.

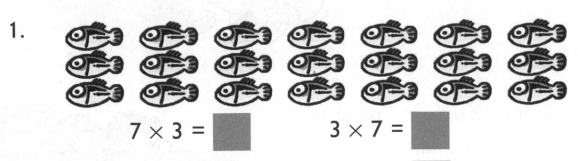

$7 \times 3 = $ ■ $3 \times 7 = $ ■

$21 \div 3 = $ ■ $21 \div 7 = $ ■

2.

Mrs. Reed bought 18 pears.
She put 6 pears in each plastic bag.
How many bags of pears were there?

3.

Jake bought 5 bundles of books.
There were 4 books in each bundle.
How many books did he buy altogether?

4.

5 children share 35 cookies equally.
How many cookies does each child get?

6

Multiplication Tables of 2 and 3

1 **Multiplication Table of 2**

Count the children by twos.

There are 2 children in each spaceship.
(a) How many children are there in 3 spaceships?

$2 \times 3 =$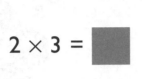

Count by twos:
2, 4, 6

There are ☐ children in 3 spaceships.

(b) How many children are there in 7 spaceships?

$2 \times 7 =$

Count by twos:
2, 4, 6, 8, 10,
12, 14

There are ☐ children in 7 spaceships.

2   4   6   8   10   12   14   16   18   20

Can you count backwards by twos?

89

1. (a) Multiply 2 by 2.

Count by twos.

$2 \times 2 = \boxed{}$

(b) Multiply 2 by 9.

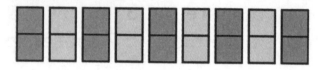

$2 \times 9 = \boxed{}$

Workbook Exercises 40 & 41

2. (a) Multiply 2 by 3.

$2 \times 3 = \boxed{}$

(b) Multiply 2 by 4.

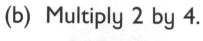

$2 \times 4 = \boxed{}$

3.

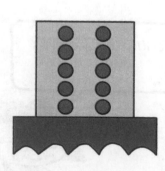

2 more

$2 \times 5 = 10$

$2 \times 6 = \boxed{}$

90

Workbook Exercise 42

4. Complete the number sentences.

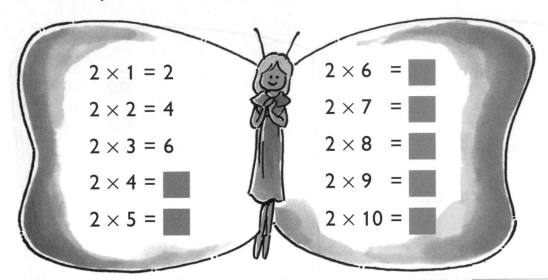

$2 \times 1 = 2$

$2 \times 2 = 4$

$2 \times 3 = 6$

$2 \times 4 = \boxed{}$

$2 \times 5 = \boxed{}$

$2 \times 6 \ = \boxed{}$

$2 \times 7 \ = \boxed{}$

$2 \times 8 \ = \boxed{}$

$2 \times 9 \ = \boxed{}$

$2 \times 10 = \boxed{}$

Workbook Exercise 43

5. (a)

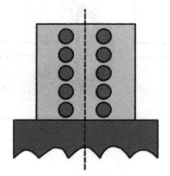

$5 + 5 = \boxed{}$

$5 \times 2 = \boxed{}$

(b)

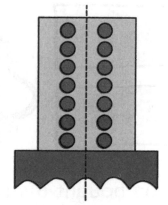

$7 + 7 = \boxed{}$

$7 \times 2 = \boxed{}$

6. (a) $8 + 8 = \boxed{}$

$8 \times 2 = \boxed{}$

(b) $9 + 9 = \boxed{}$

$9 \times 2 = \boxed{}$

91

7. Complete the number sentences.

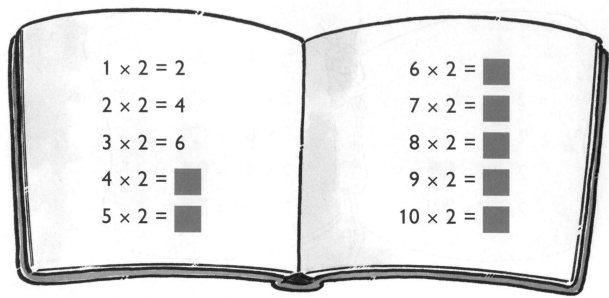

$1 \times 2 = 2$

$2 \times 2 = 4$

$3 \times 2 = 6$

$4 \times 2 = \boxed{}$

$5 \times 2 = \boxed{}$

$6 \times 2 = \boxed{}$

$7 \times 2 = \boxed{}$

$8 \times 2 = \boxed{}$

$9 \times 2 = \boxed{}$

$10 \times 2 = \boxed{}$

8. What are the missing numbers?

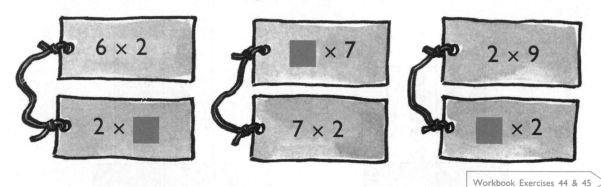

6×2

$2 \times \boxed{}$

$\boxed{} \times 7$

7×2

2×9

$\boxed{} \times 2$

Workbook Exercises 44 & 45

9. Meihua bought 6 strings.
Each string was 2 m long.
What was the total length of the strings?

2 m

$6 \times 2 = \boxed{}$

The total length was $\boxed{}$ m.

92

Workbook Exercise 46

PRACTICE 6A

Find the value of each of the following:

	(a)	(b)	(c)
1.	2×3	4×2	2×2
2.	1×2	9×2	2×8
3.	2×6	7×2	2×10
4.	5×2	3×2	2×4
5.	2×9	6×2	2×7

6. A bird has 2 wings.
   How many wings do 6 birds have?

7. At a party, each child gets 2 balloons.
   How many balloons do 10 children get?

8. Ian saves $5 a week.
   How much can he save in 2 weeks?

9. Lauren bought 4 bags of ground coffee.
   Each bag weighed 2 kg.
   How many kilograms of ground coffee did she buy?

10. Morgan made 2 sets of curtains.
    She used 8 m of cloth for each
    set of curtains.
    How many meters of cloth did
    she use altogether?

93

2 Multiplication Table of 3

Count the cars by threes.

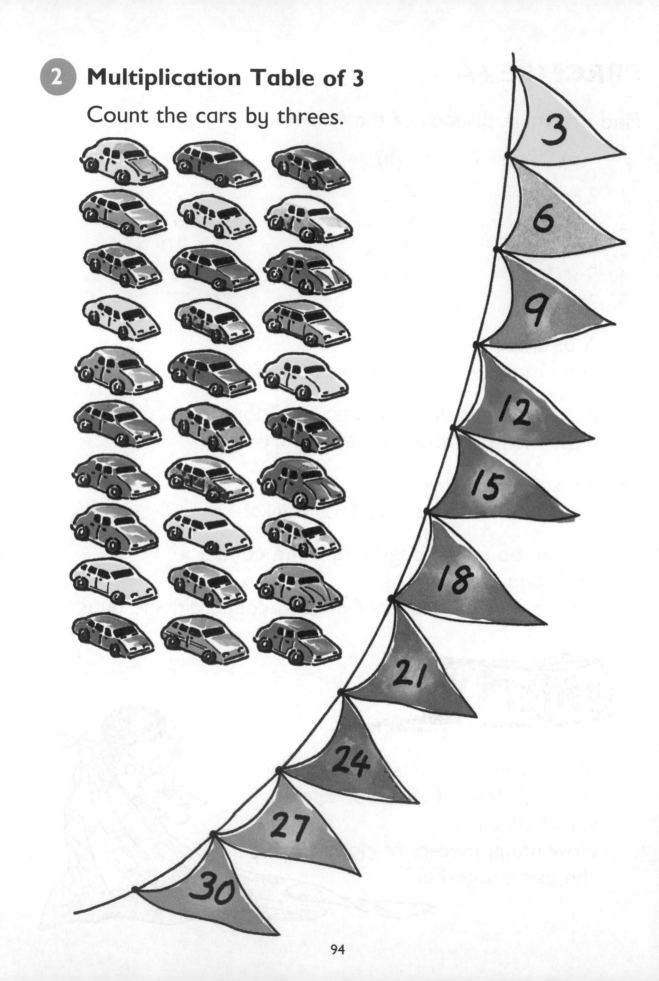

There are 3 cars in each row.
(a) How many cars are there in 5 rows?

$3 \times 5 = $ ▢

Count by threes:
3, 6, 9,
12, 15

There are ▢ cars in 5 rows.

(b) How many cars are there in 9 rows?

$3 \times 9 = $ ▢

Count by threes:
3, 6, 9,
12, 15, 18,
21, 24, 27

There are ▢ cars in 9 rows.

1. (a) Multiply 3 by 4.

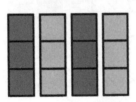

$3 \times 4 = $ ▢

Count by threes.

(b) Multiply 3 by 8.

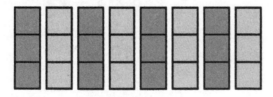

$3 \times 8 = $ ▢

95

Workbook Exercises 47 & 48

2.

$3 \times 6 = \blacksquare$

$6 \times 3 = \blacksquare$

Workbook Exercise 49

3. What are the missing numbers?

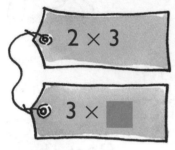 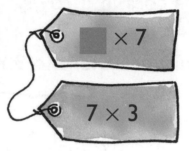 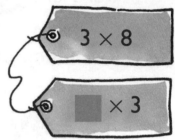

2×3

$3 \times \blacksquare$

$\blacksquare \times 7$

7×3

3×8

$\blacksquare \times 3$

4. Complete the number sentences.

$3 \times 1 = 3$

$3 \times 2 = 6$

$3 \times 3 = 9$

$3 \times 4 = \blacksquare$

$3 \times 5 = \blacksquare$

$3 \times 6 = \blacksquare$

$3 \times 7 = \blacksquare$

$3 \times 8 = \blacksquare$

$3 \times 9 = \blacksquare$

$3 \times 10 = \blacksquare$

$1 \times 3 = \blacksquare$

$2 \times 3 = \blacksquare$

$3 \times 3 = \blacksquare$

$4 \times 3 = \blacksquare$

$5 \times 3 = \blacksquare$

$6 \times 3 = \blacksquare$

$7 \times 3 = \blacksquare$

$8 \times 3 = \blacksquare$

$9 \times 3 = \blacksquare$

$10 \times 3 = \blacksquare$

Workbook Exercise 50

5.

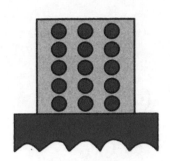

$3 \times 5 = 15$

$3 \times 6 = $ ▮

3 more

Workbook Exercise 51

6. $3 \times 10 = 30$

$3 \times 9 = 27$

$3 \times 8 = $ ▮

3 less

Workbook Exercise 52

7. Sumin bought 7 bags of sugar.
Each bag weighed 3 kg.
How many kilograms of sugar did he buy
altogether?

$7 \times 3 = $ ▮

He bought ▮ kg of sugar.

97

Workbook Exercises 53 to 55

PRACTICE 6B

Find the value of each of the following:

	(a)	(b)	(c)
1.	3×1	2×3	3×4
2.	6×3	7×3	3×8
3.	4×3	5×3	3×10
4.	3×7	9×3	3×3
5.	8×3	10×3	3×6

6. There are 3 wheels on a tricycle.
   How many wheels are there on 4 tricycles?

7. There are 7 trees in one row.
   How many trees are there in 3 rows?

8. One bag of potatoes weighs 8 kg.
   What is the weight of 3 bags of potatoes?

9. Mary made 6 dresses.
   She used 3 yd of cloth for each dress.
   How many yards of cloth did she use altogether?

10. Matthew bought 3 sets of stamps.
    There were 10 stamps in each set.
    How many stamps did he buy?

PRACTICE 6C

Find the value of each of the following:

	(a)	(b)	(c)
1.	2×1	1×3	4×2
2.	2×5	4×3	2×9
3.	8×2	3×9	3×3
4.	10×2	8×3	3×7
5.	2×7	3×5	6×3

6. Nicole can read 3 storybooks a week.
   How many storybooks can she read in 5 weeks?

7. One concert ticket costs $7.
   Mr. Banks buys 2 tickets.
   How much does he pay?

8. A bee has 6 legs.
   How many legs do 3 bees have?

9. Mrs. Lin made 9 pillow cases.
   She used 2 m of lace for each pillow case.
   How many meters of lace did she use altogether?

10. Stephanie bought 3 bags of rice flour.
    Each bag weighed 10 lb.
    How many pounds of rice flour did she buy?

99

3 Dividing by 2

Put 6 flowers equally into 2 vases.

$3 \times 2 = 6$

$6 \div 2 = \boxed{}$

Put 10 flowers equally into 2 vases.

$5 \times 2 = 10$

$10 \div 2 = \boxed{}$

100

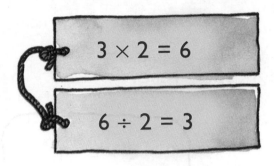

$3 \times 2 = 6$

$6 \div 2 = 3$

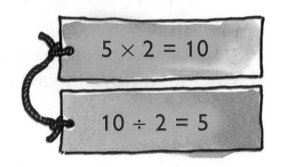

$5 \times 2 = 10$

$10 \div 2 = 5$

1. (a)

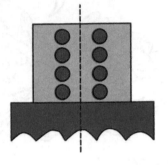

$4 \times 2 = 8$

$8 \div 2 = \boxed{}$

(b)

$7 \times 2 = 14$

$14 \div 2 = \boxed{}$

2. What are the missing numbers?

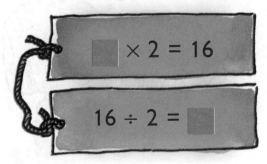

$\boxed{} \times 2 = 16$

$16 \div 2 = \boxed{}$

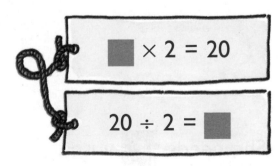

$\boxed{} \times 2 = 20$

$20 \div 2 = \boxed{}$

3. Meili has **8** flowers.
    She puts them equally into 2 vases.
    How many flowers are there in each vase?

$$8 \div 2 = \boxed{}$$

■ × 2 = 8

There are ▨ flowers in each vase.

4. Siti has **14** flowers.
    She wants to put 2 flowers in a vase.
    How many vases does she need?

$$14 \div 2 = \boxed{}$$

■ × 2 = 14

She needs ▨ vases.

102

5. Kristi has a string **12 m** long.
   She cuts it into equal pieces.
   Each piece is **2 m** long.
   How many pieces of string does she get?

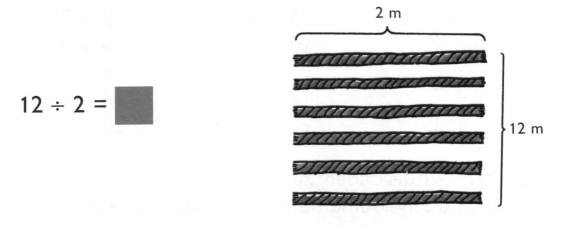

$12 \div 2 = \boxed{}$

She gets $\boxed{}$ pieces of string.

6. Justin has a string **18 m** long.
   He cuts it into **2** equal pieces.
   How long is each piece?

$18 \div 2 = \boxed{}$

Each piece is $\boxed{}$ m long.

103

Workbook Exercise 57

PRACTICE 6D

Find the value of each of the following:

	(a)	(b)	(c)
1.	4×2	5×2	2×2
2.	$8 \div 2$	$10 \div 2$	$4 \div 2$
3.	6×2	9×2	8×2
4.	$12 \div 2$	$18 \div 2$	$16 \div 2$
5.	$14 \div 2$	$2 \div 2$	$20 \div 2$

6. Nathan arranged 20 chairs in 2 rows.
   He put the same number of chairs in each row.
   How many chairs were there in each row?

7. Dan saved $2 a day.
   How many days did he take to save $18?

8. Mrs. Ricci bought 2 kg of grapes.
   1 kg of grapes cost $5.
   How much did she pay for the grapes?

9. Kevin had a rope 16 m long.
   He cut it into 2 equal pieces.
   Find the length of each piece.

10. Nicole makes 14 pies.
    She wants to put 2 pies in a box.
    How many boxes does she need?

4 Dividing by 3

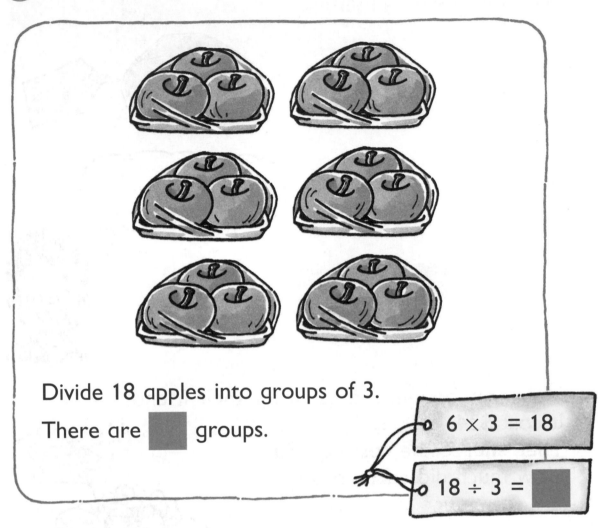

Divide 18 apples into groups of 3.

There are ▢ groups.

$6 \times 3 = 18$

$18 \div 3 = ▢$

1. What are the missing numbers?

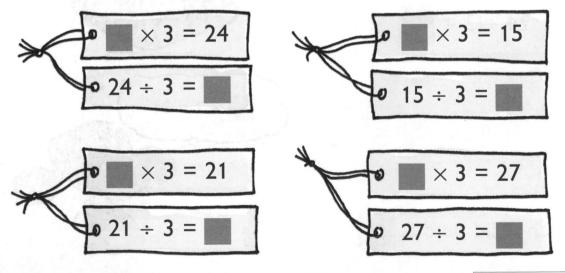

▢ $\times 3 = 24$

$24 \div 3 = ▢$

▢ $\times 3 = 15$

$15 \div 3 = ▢$

▢ $\times 3 = 21$

$21 \div 3 = ▢$

▢ $\times 3 = 27$

$27 \div 3 = ▢$

105

Workbook Exercise 58

2. Mr. Wang bought 30 apples at 3 for $1.
   How much did he pay?

$30 \div 3 =$ ☐

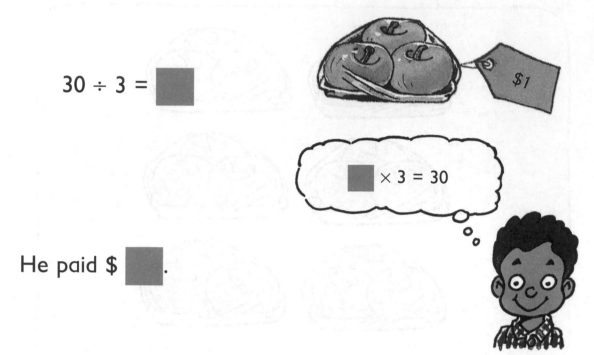

☐ $\times 3 = 30$

He paid $ ☐ .

3. 3 children bought a present for their friend.
   It cost $24.
   They shared the cost equally.
   How much did each child pay?

$24 \div 3 =$ ☐

☐ $\times 3 = 24$

Each child paid $ ☐ .

106

Workbook Exercises 59 to 62

PRACTICE 6E

Find the value of each of the following:

	(a)	(b)	(c)
1.	4×3	6×3	5×3
2.	$12 \div 3$	$18 \div 3$	$15 \div 3$
3.	9×3	7×3	8×3
4.	$27 \div 3$	$21 \div 3$	$24 \div 3$
5.	$9 \div 3$	$6 \div 3$	$30 \div 3$

6. Ricardo packed 30 bottles equally into 3 boxes.
   How many bottles were there in each box?

7. Devi paid $18 for 3 kg of cherries.
   Find the cost of 1 kg of cherries.

8. David had 15 toy soldiers.
   He lined them up in 3 rows.
   There were the same number of soldiers in each row.
   How many toy soldiers were there in each row?

9. Matthew bought 9 books.
   Each book cost $3.
   How much did he pay altogether?

10. There are 24 beads on 3 strings.
    There are the same number of beads on each string.
    How many beads are there on each string?

PRACTICE 6F

Find the value of each of the following:

	(a)	(b)	(c)
1.	$10 \div 2$	$14 \div 2$	$8 \div 2$
2.	$9 \div 3$	$15 \div 3$	$12 \div 3$
3.	$12 \div 2$	$16 \div 2$	$20 \div 2$
4.	$18 \div 3$	$24 \div 3$	$21 \div 3$
5.	$18 \div 2$	$30 \div 3$	$27 \div 3$

6. Emily had a piece of ribbon 24 cm long.
   She cut it into 3 equal pieces.
   Find the length of each piece.

7. Sam saved $3 a week.
   How many weeks did he take to save $30?

8. The watermelon weighs 7 kg.
   How much does it cost?

9. A shopkeeper packed 16 kg of flour into bags.
   Each bag weighed 2 kg.
   How many bags did he get?

10. Mr. Chen bought 18 pears.
    How much did he pay?

108

REVIEW B

1. Write the numbers.
   (a) Six hundred six
   (b) Eight hundred fifty-five
   (c) Four hundred forty

2. Write these numbers in words.
   (a) 250   (b) 744   (c) 307   (d) 922

3. (a) What number is 10 more than 203?
   (b) What number is 100 more than 349?
   (c) What number is 1 less than 800?
   (d) What number is 100 less than 425?

4. What are the missing numbers?
   (a) 3, 6, 9, 12, ▢ , ▢ , ▢ , 24, ▢ , 30
   (b) 500, 490, 480, ▢ , ▢ , ▢ , 440, ▢ , 420

5. Arrange these numbers in order.
   Begin with the smallest.

   928   930   912

6. Find the missing numbers.
   (a) 70 + ▢ = 78   (b) 200 + ▢ = 208
   (c) 400 + ▢ = 490   (d) 400 + ▢ = 409
   (e) 578 − ▢ = 508   (f) 695 − ▢ = 690
   (g) 794 − ▢ = 694   (h) 999 − ▢ = 949

7. (a)

   (b)

   The watermelon weighs ▢ kg.

   The vegetables weigh ▢ g.

8.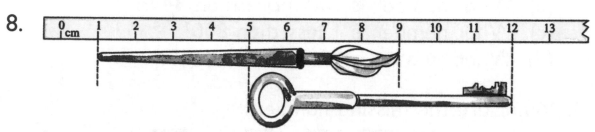

   Which is longer, the brush or the key?
   How much longer?

9. Bonita bought some apples for $5. How many apples did she buy?

3 for $1

10. There are 128 boys.
    There are 25 more girls than boys.
    How many girls are there?

11. Mary is 142 cm tall.
    She is 14 cm taller than her brother.
    Find the height of her brother.

12. Mrs. Goodman made 24 cream puffs for a party.
    She placed 3 cream puffs on a plate.
    How many plates did she use?

110

REVIEW C

Find the value of each of the following:

	(a)	(b)	(c)
1.	400 + 8	500 + 90	375 + 180
2.	678 − 600	798 − 95	920 − 186
3.	2 × 9	3 × 8	8 × 2
4.	18 ÷ 2	24 ÷ 3	16 ÷ 2
5.	21 ÷ 3	20 ÷ 2	30 ÷ 3

6. What is the missing number in each ■ ?

   (a) 600 + 80 + 9 = ■   (b) 500 + 5 = ■

   (c) 300 + ■ = 340   (d) 700 + ■ + 6 = 706

7. Write > or < in place of each ●.

   (a) 309 ● 390   (b) 410 ● 408

   (c) 18 ● 16   (d) 85 ● 100

8.

   (a) The pear weighs ■ g.

   (b) The apple weighs ■ g.

111

9. The chart shows the number of members in a chess club.
   How many members are there in the chess club?

Men : 128
Women : 94
Children : 46

10. Tasha wants to buy this violin.
    She has only $89.
    How much more money does she need?

$120

11. Mrs. Gray bought 3 boxes of cakes.
    There were 6 cakes in each box.
    How many cakes did she buy?

12. 3 children shared $27 equally.
    How much money did each child receive?

13. There are 820 rubber trees.
    There are 95 more coconut trees than rubber trees.
    How many coconut trees are there?

14. Jordan has $145.
    He needs $65 more to buy this camera.
    How much does the camera cost?

15. A tailor used 18 m of cloth to make shirts.
    He used 2 m of cloth for each shirt.
    How many shirts did he make?